The One Minute Manager® Builds High Performing Teams

Also by Ken Blanchard

Gung Ho!: Turn on the People in Any Organization (with Sheldon Bowles), 1998

Raving Fans: A Revolutionary Approach to Customer Service (with Sheldon Bowles), 1993

Managing by Values (with Michael O'Connor), 1997

Mission Possible (with Terry Waghorn), 1996

Management of Organizational Behavior: Utilizing Human Resources (with Paul Hersey), 7th Edition, 1996

Empowerment Takes More Than a Minute (with John P. Carlos and Alan Randolph), 1996

Everyone's a Coach (with Don Shula), 1995

We Are the Beloved, 1994

The One Minute Manager Meets the Monkey (with William Oncken, Jr., and Hal Burrows), 1989

The Power of Ethical Management (with Norman Vincent Peale), 1988

Leadership and the One Minute Manager (with Patricia Zigarmi and Drea Zigarmi), 1985

Organizational Change Through Effective Leadership (with Robert H. Guest and Paul Hersey), 2nd Edition, 1985

Putting the One Minute Manager to Work (with Robert Lorber), 1984

The One Minute Manager (with Spencer Johnson), 1982

The Family Game: A Situational Approach to Effective Parenting (with Paul Hersey), 1979

The One Minute Manager Builds High Performing Teams

Ken Blanchard
Donald Carew
Eunice Parisi-Carew

WILLIAM MORROW AND COMPANY, INC.

NEW YORK

It is the policy of William Morrow and Company, Inc., and its imprints and
affiliates, recognizing the importance of preserving what has been written,
to print the books we publish on acid-free paper, and we exert our best
efforts to that end.

The Library of Congress has cataloged a previous
edition of this title.

Library of Congress Cataloging-in-Publication Data

Blanchard, Kenneth H.
The one minute manager builds high performing teams / Kenneth
Blanchard, Donald Carew, Eunice Parisi-Carew.
p.   cm.
ISBN 0-688-10972-1
1. Work groups. I. Carew, Donald II. Parisi-Carew. Eunice. III. Title
[HD66.B55 1991]
658.4'02—dc20   91-18718
                                                                CIP

Revised Edition ISBN 0-688-17215-6

Printed in the United States of America

Revised Edition 2000

5   6   7   8   9   10

www.williammorrow.com

 *The Symbol*

The One Minute Manager's symbol—a one minute readout from the face of a modern digital watch—is intended to remind each of us to take a minute out of our day to look into the faces of the people we manage. And to realize that *they* are our most important resources.

Introduction

Never before in the history of the workplace has the concept of teamwork been more important to the functioning of successful organizations. With the rapid social, technological and informational changes that are occurring, our society is faced with stresses never before encountered. Our organizations are more complex and more competitive. No longer can we depend upon a few peak performers to rise to the top to lead. If we are to survive we must figure out ways to tap into the creativity and potential of people at all levels.

Couple these changes with a shifting population, a global economy, a change in values and a change in the traditional work ethic, and you have a rising demand for new organizational structures and a new definition of leadership. People are demanding more. They want fulfillment as well as good pay.

As a result, there has been a movement toward participation and involvement so strong that it's called the *Third Revolution* in management practices. A new organizational structure has come into its own—the team which increases ownership and commitment, unleashes creativity and builds skills. Today's leader must be an enabler of people and a facilitator of teams—not only as an effective team leader but as an effective team member as well.

The team of The Ken Blanchard Companies has been doing a great deal of work in the area of high performing teams for the past twenty years, and founding Blanchard associates, Don Carew and Eunice Parisi-Carew, have spearheaded that work. Don and Eunice have been close friends and colleagues for over thirty years and we have spent countless hours working together on the implementation of the concepts in this book. I believe the concepts taught through parable in *The One Minute Manager® Builds High Performing Teams* present a clear map for managing the journey to more productive and satisfying teams.

As you'll see, our work on teams is well integrated with Situational Leadership® II *(Leadership and the One Minute Manager®)*. In fact, improvements made to the Situational Leadership® model were stimulated by our research on group development, and I am indebted to Don and Eunice for advocating many of those changes. Their commitment to creating opportunities for people to have more satisfying and productive lives and for organizations to be more caring, creative and successful is at the heart of their work.

The ideas in this latest edition to THE ONE MINUTE MANAGER® LIBRARY have been shared with thousands of people in all types of teams and organizations and these concepts never fail to have a powerful impact. I hope this book is as informative and helpful to you and your teams as it has been to them.

Ken Blanchard
Coauthor
The One Minute Manager®

To our mothers

Dorothy, Marjorie and Jenny,

who gave us our first lessons in

empowerment and

loving others

Contents

The One Minute Manager Receives a Call   1
The Problem   3
The Importance of Groups   6
Characteristics of a High Performing Team   9
The Importance of Vision   16
Diagnosis   19
Understanding Group Dynamics   21
Stage 1: Orientation   26
Stage 2: Dissatisfaction   35
Stage 4: Production   45
Stage 3: Integration   52
Changes in Productivity and Morale   59
Adaptability   62
Four Leadership Styles   65
Task and Maintenance Functions   69
Teaching Someone Else   71
Using the Concepts   74
Answering the Questions   77
Managing the Journey to Empowerment   79
When to Change One's Leadership Style   83
Regression   90
Process Observation   91
Understanding Group Dynamics   95
The Manager as Educator   96
The New One Minute Managers   100
Sharing It with Others   102
Praisings   106
About the Authors   108
Services Available   112

THE One Minute Manager was staring out his office window. It was still his favorite place to come when he wanted to think. As he gazed across the grounds, the sound of the phone ringing startled him. Coming back to reality, he walked over to the coffee table in front of his couch and picked up the receiver. When he was in his office the One Minute Manager liked to answer his own phone.

The voice on the other end of the phone was Dan Brockway, the director of training at a large chemical company.

"How's it going, Dan?" asked the One Minute Manager.

"Just fine," said Dan, "but I do need some advice on our Essentials of Management course."

The Essentials of Management course was a new training program that Dan was teaching at his company that focused on the key skills managers needed to be effective in the new millennium. He had spent some time with the One Minute Manager while he was designing the course and was enthusiastic about the commitment of his company's top management to expose all their managers to the best management thinking available.

"Didn't you just finish the first session?"

"I sure did," said Dan. "And the reviews were great with one exception. A young woman, Maria Sanchez, who coordinates our customer service programs, has some serious concerns about the usefulness of some of the materials. In fact, she wrote me a letter about her concerns and distributed copies to key people."

"What were her concerns?" asked the One Minute Manager.

66 SHE said all the concepts taught focused primarily on managing people one-on-one and, as such, are limited. She claims that 50 to 90 percent of most managers' time is spent in some form of group activity with two or more people, and yet our course doesn't emphasize teamwork at all. Therefore, we are not providing help in one of the most significant areas of a manager's job."

"That's interesting," said the One Minute Manager. "Tell me more."

"She also thinks the concepts of One Minute Management are based too much on control," said Dan. "The manager sets the goals, the manager gives praisings and the manager delivers reprimands. Let me quote from her letter:

'We need managers who can foster teamwork, facilitate group problem solving and focus the group's attention and enthusiasm on continuous improvement. In today's world, group productivity is more important than individual task accomplishment. The success of individual managers should depend on how well the manager's team improves in quality and productivity on a continuous basis. Systems that can pit team player against team player must be changed so that the priority of each team member becomes the accomplishment of the team's mission. To do that, managers must give up a great deal of control to their people. When that occurs, a feeling of team ownership is created and the team develops pride that comes from producing high quality accomplishments. You will never hear "It's not my job" in an organization committed to teamwork.' "

"She sounds like quite a person," said the One Minute Manager. "How can I help you?"

"Could you dictate a response to her letter? She could really disrupt our whole program if we don't get her on track."

"I don't think she's off track," said the One Minute Manager. "In fact, I'd like to meet her. Sounds like she is really aware of some important issues. I think that One Minute Management principles are sound, but I would agree with her that if you teach those principles without any attention to group skills, you have given managers only half the story. Let's have lunch tomorrow at 12:30 in the main dining room of City Hotel so I can explain to you why I think Maria is on the *right* track."

"That would be fine with me," said Dan. "Sounds like I still have some things to learn."

"Don't feel like the Lone Ranger," said The One Minute Manager. "See you tomorrow!"

THE next day at lunch, the One Minute Manager immediately got to the reason for the meeting.

"Dan, I used to be frustrated at work even though I knew all kinds of effective management techniques. For a long time I didn't know why I was frustrated. I finally realized one day, just as your friend Maria has realized, that most of my job was not supervising and working with people one-on-one but, instead, it involved working with people in groups."

"I thought a lot about what you said last night," commented Dan. "So you really don't believe that we spend much time supervising people individually?"

"No, I don't," said the One Minute Manager. "In fact, most managers spend less than 30 percent of their time directly supervising their people individually. They spend most of their time in group meetings dealing with their people or with peers and their boss, or with people external to their organization such as customers or suppliers. When I first realized that, I decided that I'd better learn something about groups and how they operate."

"Could you tell me what you learned?" asked Dan.

"First of all," said the One Minute Manager, "when groups are operating effectively they can solve more complex problems, make better decisions, release more creativity and do more to build individual skills and commitment than individuals working alone."

"Can't they also destroy productivity?" wondered Dan.

"They sure can," said the One Minute Manager, "if they're not managed well. That's why today's leader must be an enabler of people and a facilitator of teams."

"What else did you learn?"

"Secondly, all groups are unique," continued the One Minute Manager.

"They are all dynamic, complex, ever-changing, living systems that—just like individuals—have behavior patterns and lives of their own."

"How do groups differ from one another?" asked Dan.

"Well, there are the obvious differences of size, purpose and individual members, but an important difference that is often overlooked is in their stage of development," said the One Minute Manager. "All groups go through similar stages as they grow from a collection of individuals when they first get together to a smoothly functioning, effective team."

"Do you mean all groups go through the same stages of development no matter what their purpose or size or how frequently they meet?" asked Dan.

"In general, yes, but primarily I'm thinking about teams that interact face-to-face on a regular basis, have a relatively constant membership of between 2 to 15 members and are working together on a common task or problem. They can be ongoing work units, special task forces or committees with short-term objectives, athletic teams or even social groups or families," answered the One Minute Manager.

"That certainly would include most of the groups to which I've belonged," said Dan. "But what about larger groups?"

"The same stages can be observed in larger groups as well," said the One Minute Manager, "but when groups get larger than 15 or 20 people, they become less effective and should divide into smaller units to accomplish tasks or solve problems."

"That makes sense," said Dan. "Can you tell me how you would describe an effective team?"

"BEFORE I answer that," said the One Minute Manager, "I'd like you to think of a time when you were part of an outstanding team or group. Think of a team that produced a high-quality result and one to which you were proud to belong."

"There haven't been many like that," replied Dan, "but the design team I've been working with for this Essentials of Management course comes close. Five of us have been working together for the past six months and we feel good about what we are accomplishing."

"What I'd like you to do," said the One Minute Manager, "is think about that team and make a list of the factors you think have contributed to its effectiveness. I have a phone call to make, so let's get back together in 10 minutes and see what you have on your list."

"Fine," said Dan as he began to make notes.

After the phone call the One Minute Manager asked Dan to show him his list.

"It's not very long," remarked Dan, "but I think it describes some of the main characteristics of the effective groups with which I have worked." Dan had seven items on his list:

1. I know what I have to do and the team's goals are clear.
2. Everyone takes some responsibility for leadership.
3. There is active participation by everyone.
4. I feel appreciated and supported by others.
5. Team members listen when I speak.
6. Different opinions are respected.
7. We enjoy working together and we have fun.

"That's a good start, Dan," said the One Minute Manager, "and it's right on target with what I've observed happening in high-performing teams. I've come up with the acronym PERFORM, which describes the essentials of an effective team. I've had it put on a small card so people can keep it with them at all times." With that, the One Minute Manager reached into his coat pocket to get a card and then handed it to Dan. It read:

Characteristics of
High Performing Teams

Purpose and Values
Empowerment
Relationships and Communication
Flexibility
Optimal Performance
Recognition and Appreciation
Morale

"That's catchy," said Dan. "I'd be interested in how you describe those variables."

"Sure," said the One Minute Manager as he handed Dan a questionnaire. "Here's a rating form that I put together which describes each of the characteristics and permits you to evaluate a team to which you belong. As you read it think about your design team."

Dan began to read:

Purpose and Values
1. The team has a clear commitment to a common purpose. Team members know what the team's work is and why it is important.
2. Common values and norms promote integrity, quality and collaboration.
3. Specific team goals are clear, challenging, agreed on and relevant to the purpose.
4. Strategies for achieving goals are clear and agreed on.
5. Individual roles are clear, and their relationship to the team purpose and goals is understood.

Empowerment
6. Values, norms and policies encourage initiative, involvement and creativity.
7. All relevant organization and business information is readily available to the team.
8. The team has the authority, within understood boundaries, to take action and make decisions.
9. Direction, structure and training are available to support individual and team development.
10. The team is committed to the continuing growth and development of all team members.

Relationships and Communication
11. Different ideas, opinions, feelings and perspectives from all team members are encouraged and considered.
12. Team members listen actively to each other for understanding, not judgment.
13. Methods of managing conflict and finding common ground are understood.
14. Cultural differences including race, gender, nationality, age, etc., are valued and respected.
15. Honest and caring feedback helps team members to be aware of their strengths and weaknesses.

Flexibility

16. Team members share responsibility for team development and leadership.
17. The team is able to meet challenges using the unique talents and strengths of all team members.
18. Team members shift from behaviors that provide direction or support as needed.
19. The team is open to exploring different ways of doing things and adapts to change.
20. Calculated risks are supported. Mistakes are seen as opportunities for learning.

Optimal Performance

21. The team constantly produces significant results; the job gets done.
22. The team is committed to high standards and measures for productivity, quality and service.
23. The team is committed to learning from mistakes and to continuous improvement.
24. Effective problem-solving and decision-making skills overcome obstacles and promote creativity.
25. The team coordinates efforts with other teams, vendors and customers as appropriate.

Recognition and Appreciation

26. Individual and team accomplishments are often acknowledged by team leaders and team members.
27. Team members have a sense of personal accomplishment in relation to task contributions.
28. Team contributions are valued and recognized by the larger organization.
29. Team members feel highly regarded within the team.
30. The team celebrates successes and milestones.

Morale

31. Team members are confident and enthusiastic about the team's efforts and are committed to success.
32. The team encourages hard work, as well as having fun.
33. There is a strong sense of pride in and satisfaction with the team's work.
34. There is a strong sense of trust and team spirit among team members.
35. Team members have developed supportive and caring relationships and help each other.

"Thanks," said Dan as he looked up from the rating form. "This is really helpful. I would rate our design team 4 or 5 on every one of those scales.

"We had a clear purpose, we felt empowered, our relationships and communication were good, we were flexible, our quality and performance were high, we felt appreciated and recognized and our morale was strong. It's sad, though, that I can't say that about most of the groups with which I've worked."

"Yes, it is sad," said the One Minute Manager. "Wouldn't it be wonderful if all of our work units could describe themselves as PERFORM teams."

"It sure would," Dan replied. "If that were true, morale and productivity would go off the chart. I saw a poster on a school bulletin board that captured the importance of developing a team. It stated:

*

NONE OF US

IS AS SMART

AS ALL OF US

*

"How true that is," said the One Minute Manager. "And if we acted on that belief, think what a difference it would make in how people feel about themselves and their work. And that's what people are demanding today. They want fulfillment as well as good pay."

"Are any of the PERFORM characteristics more important than any other?"

"No," said the One Minute Manager. "They all have different functions. An effective team starts with a clear *purpose* and a set of values. The hoped-for end results are *optimal productivity* and good *morale*. The means to those ends are *empowerment, relationships* and *communication, flexibility* and *recognition* and *appreciation*.

"So the first thing an effective leader needs to do is create a common purpose that helps point the team in the right direction," suggested Dan.

"That's essential," said the One Minute Manager. "A common purpose tells people what they are trying to accomplish and why they are working together. It creates meaning and helps everyone row in the same direction. The team also needs to agree on a set of values that will guide the team's choices and determine how the team pursues its purpose. I can't say enough about the importance of purpose and values. One wise organization philosopher put it this way:

The only thing

which will ultimately

hold any organization together

will be a shared conviction

in its purpose and its methods. *

*Charles Handy, "The Sixth Need of Business: 'Wisdom from an Oarsman,' " Rediscovering the Soul of Business, Zukav ed., et al. San Francisco: New Leaders Press, 1995.

"I recently read a beautiful story that relates to the importance of purpose and values. Two workers were hammering on a piece of granite with a sledgehammer. When asked what he was doing the first worker said, 'I'm just trying to make a living cracking this granite.'

"When asked the same question, the second worker said, 'I want to make a difference. I'm part of a team building a cathedral.' "

"Purpose inspires performance and commitment," said the One Minute Manager. "Knowing where you are headed and having everything move in the same direction is critical. But alignment around shared purpose and values is just the beginning of the road to a high performing team."

"That's what I was afraid of," said Dan thoughtfully. "Knowing how a high performing team functions is helpful, but how groups get to that point is a mystery to me."

"Well," replied the One Minute Manager, "it isn't by accident! And it's not as much of a mystery as it once was. We have learned a lot about group dynamics, group development and group leadership over the past 50 years. It is just that most organizations haven't put that knowledge to use very effectively. We have only recently realized how powerful teams can be in improving productivity, quality and human satisfaction in organizations."

"I'M sold," said Dan. "What do I need to do to be an effective team leader and how can I help my people over time?"

"The whole process of developing a high performing team involves three major skills on the part of team leaders and team members as well. The first is *Diagnosis*, the second is *Adaptability* and the third is *Empowerment*.

"Let's start with Diagnosis," continued the One Minute Manager. "Understanding the dynamics and the behavioral patterns that exist in groups is essential if you want to facilitate the team's development and productivity. I have found that the skillful leader or team member must do more than listen and talk. Perhaps most important is the skill of observing the team in action. Groups are extremely complex. As you increase the size of the group, the number of interaction patterns or subgroups flows geometrically so that with two people in a group there is just one subgroup. With four people in a team it jumps to 11 subgroups and with eight people it goes to 247 subgroups. Because of this complexity it is important that we have ways to observe the group that help us make sense of what is going on."

"I see!" exclaimed Dan. "Thinking about it that way makes it seem almost impossible to ever make sense of what goes on in a team."

Elements of Group/Team Interaction

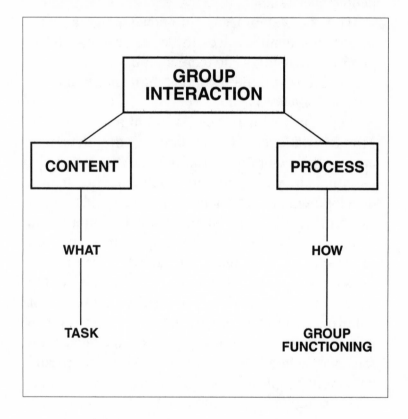

66"THE *content* is what the group is doing—its task," said the One Minute Manager. "For example, if later today someone asked you what went on during our lunch together, you would tell them we talked about the importance and characteristics of groups. We were all trained in school to track content and ignore process. Content describes *what* was done at a meeting, while process depicts *how* the group functions. The process is what is happening to and between group members, like leadership struggle, communication and the ways decisions are made. You have to focus on it to see it. Unfortunately we often pay little attention to process, yet it is critically important because process affects outcome. Group leaders who do not legitimize looking at group process can become blind to why people are unhappy even though the agenda at the meeting is getting accomplished. When that happens, 'I should have said' meetings begin to crop up in the hallways, bathrooms, stairwells, elevators and parking lots."

"This list is a helpful reminder to me whenever I am observing a group's process." The One Minute Manager wrote on his note pad again. When he finished he ripped off the sheet. It read:

*

WHAT TO OBSERVE
IN GROUPS

—*Communication and
participation*
—*Decision making*
—*Conflict*
—*Leadership*
—*Goals and roles*
—*Group norms*
—*Problem solving*
—*Group climate*
—*Individual behavior*

*

"*Communication* and *participation*," continued the One Minute Manager, "are about who talks to whom? Who is left out? Who talks most often? etc. *Decision making* involves how a group goes about selecting a course of action—majority rule, consensus, lack of response, etc. *Conflict* is inevitable and necessary in reaching effective and creative solutions for problems. How is conflict handled in the group—avoidance, compromise, competition, collaboration, etc. *Leadership* is all about who is influencing whom. To be effective a team must be clear on its *roles* (who does what?) and *goals* (what are they trying to accomplish?). *Norms* are the assumptions or expectations held by group members that govern the kinds of behaviors that are appropriate or inappropriate in the group. They are the ground rules which regulate the group's behavior. Which norms are most obvious in this group? Effective *problem solving* involves identifying and formulating the problem, generating alternative solutions, analyzing consequences, action planning and evaluation. How does the group solve problems? *Group climate* refers to the feeling or tone of the group—how pleasant it seems." And finally *individual behavior* focuses on what team members are doing to help accomplish the task(s) and/or help the group functioning. Sometimes individual members get self-oriented—they focus on their own needs rather than group needs. It's important to identify when that is occurring too.

"That's a lot to be watching," said Dan, "if you are also a member of the group."

"That's true," said the One Minute Manager. "But all group leaders, and group members as well, need to practice the skill of being a participant observer."

"What is that?" asked Dan.

"That means being fully engaged in the content or the agenda, whatever it is, and yet being able to step back and observe the dynamics which are occurring in the group at the same time," said the One Minute Manager.

"So, for example, if we are making a decision I need to be involved in the decision itself, as well as be aware of how the decision is being made," replied Dan.

"Absolutely right," said the One Minute Manager. "If a decision is railroaded through by one or two members and not checked for agreement, you may find yourself up a creek without a paddle and have little support when you go to implement the decision."

"I've certainly seen that happen," smiled Dan.

"It sounds tough, though, to be both participant and observer."

"It is at first, but the skill of participant observer is just like any other human skill. It can be learned and practiced until it is second nature," replied the One Minute Manager.

"Sounds like a challenge," said Dan.

"Yes it is," said the One Minute Manager. "It takes concentration and practice. That starts with learning to observe and track the dynamics which occur in a group setting. Understanding those dynamics is the key to diagnosing a group's functioning and the stage of its development."

Dan got to do some group observation on Monday afternoon. The One Minute Manager arranged for him to sit in on a performance appraisal task force chaired by Ron Tilman, the company's chief operating officer.

Dan arrived a few moments early for the meeting on Monday to find all members already there drinking coffee and chatting amiably. Smiling, he joined the conversation, which ended promptly at 2:00 p.m., when a jovial-looking man in his early fifties entered the room. He immediately went to Dan and stuck out his hand. "Good afternoon. I'm Ron Tilman. Glad you could make it."

After exchanging greetings with team members and introducing Dan to the rest of the group, Ron started the meeting.

"I'm excited about this task force. I see this as a very important team that could have a major impact on our organization. We are charged with revising our performance appraisal system so that it is more helpful in creating higher levels of motivation and performance throughout our organization. A successful system should help all people set clearer goals, know how they are doing in relation to those goals, and provide a framework for providing reviews and recognition for accomplishment. It should help managers be more effective in developing competence and commitment among their staff."

"My hope," continued Ron, "is that what we develop will help this company be a win-win organization for our people and for our customers. It is a complex task and we will need to learn how to work together, be open in our communication, share leadership and decision-making responsibilities and build ourselves into a high-performing team."

"We have a one-month window to accomplish this task. The first step is to clarify our mission and to come to agreement on the goals and the roles each of you will play in its accomplishment."

Ron proceeded to write the roles and goals of the team on a flipchart at the head of the table.

Dan was struck with the efficiency of the meeting opening, but a bit disturbed about the directness of Tilman. He observed the eagerness of the team and, although he felt their expectations were a bit unrealistic (such as the fact that they thought they could accomplish the task in one month), he was surprised that Tilman did not encourage their enthusiasm as the meeting progressed, but instead kept pulling them back to the task.

After the meeting Dan approached Tilman. "Well, what did you think about our first meeting?" asked Tilman.

"To be honest, I'm not sure," replied Dan. "I liked the way you gave them the big picture and how you got things started. But I also noticed people expressing some concern about the task, and some members seemed tense."

"Yes," said Ron. "Whenever you have a new team, members are concerned about how they fit into the team. This causes some caution and mistrust between team members. You can expect a combination of caution and excitement at first. What did you think about my leadership style?"

"Well," smiled Dan, "you were a bit direct. More so than I would have expected, but it seemed to work. It did not hamper their enthusiasm. In fact, they seemed somewhat relieved."

"Do you think they have a firm foundation to start from?" questioned Tilman.

"They sure do," replied Dan. "I think they have an overall sense of purpose and are beginning to understand their goals and roles and operating ground rules."

"That's what I wanted," smiled Tilman. "All new teams need to have a sense of purpose as well as some clarity about team values and goals, individual roles, team norms and decision making procedures. I'm pleased you saw that happening. Thanks for joining us."

When Dan went to see the One Minute Manager later that afternoon he was asked, "Well, how was your visit with the performance review task force?"

"It was fine, I guess," said Dan. "Your comments about creating a common purpose sure held up. Ron spent some time outlining a purpose and his hopes. Everyone seemed to be eager, but they needed some sense of direction. Ron clearly provided that kind of leadership. If that's your secret to building a high performing team then I got it—the leader should take charge."

"It's not quite that simple," said the One Minute Manager. "Remember, that was the first meeting of that task force and the members needed to be clear on their mission, goals and responsibilities. All teams go through stages in their development and you've just described what is pretty typical for a team in its first stage. I call that the *Orientation* Stage or Stage 1. This card will summarize what's going on in Stage 1."

When the One Minute Manager handed Dan the card he read:

Stage 1—Orientation

Characteristics
- Moderate eagerness
- High, often unrealistic expectations
- Anxiety about roles, acceptance, trust in others, demands on them
- Tentative, polite, conforming behavior
- Lack of clarity about purpose, norms, roles, goals, structure (how they will work together)
- Dependent on authority for direction and support
- Some testing of boundaries

Needs
- A common understanding of the team's purpose
- Agreement on values and norms for working together
- Agreement on roles, goals and standards
- Agreement on decision-making authority and accountability
- Agreement on structure and boundaries—how work will get done and by whom, timelines, tasks and required skills
- Information about available resources
- Knowledge about each other to utilize diverse talents and build personal connections

Issues
- Personal well-being
- Acceptance
- Trust

"It looks like Stage 1 is really important," said Dan. "There seem to be a lot of needs that have to be met."

"You are absolutely right," said the One Minute Manager. "This is the stage when the team needs to develop a team charter that creates a solid foundation for the future work of the team and makes sure that all the needs will be satisfied."

"I would imagine," said Dan, "that most teams either neglect to develop a clear charter or do only a superficial job."

"Absolutely," said the One Minute Manager. "Because it is so important we have created a model for building a team charter."

The Team Charter Model

The Team Charter is a set of agreements that clearly states what the team wants to accomplish, why it is important and how the team will work together to achieve results.

Organizational Vision, Purpose and Values are the hub of the team charter. They provide the context for the team's existence.

The **Team Vision, Purpose and Values** must be in alignment with those of the organization. The **Vision** is a picture of the ideal end result. The **Purpose** identifies the work of the team and why it is important. It provides the direction for assigning roles, setting goals and determining strategies. **Values** are the enduring beliefs that guide the team's actions.

Team Norms are ground rules that identify appropriate behaviors for team members.

Team Member Roles define individual responsibilities for the successful operation of the team.

Key Responsibility Areas (KRAs) and Goals are derived from the team's purpose. KRAs define the major functional areas involved in achieving the team's prupose. Goals identify the measurable outcomes and timelines that are needed to be successful.

Communication Strategies ensure timely sharing of information among team members, stakeholders and the organization.

Decision Making is the process the team uses to make decisions. **Authority** defines the scope of the team's responsibility in decision making. **Accountability** establishes strategies to ensure that commitments are kept.

Resources are the tangible materials and support needed by the team to accomplish its goals.

Team Norms

Team Member Roles

Key Responsibility Areas and Goals

Team Vision, Purpose and Values

Organizational Vision, Purpose and Values

Communication Strategies

Resources

Decision Making, Authority and Accountability

The Team Charter Leader's Guide. Escondido, CA. Blanchard Training and Development, Inc., 1998.

After reading the model summary Dan said, "Wow, if a team really follows this model, they should be off to a great start."

"Yes," said the One Minute Manager. "Since we began using this process we have found that our teams come together much more quickly even though it takes time at the beginning."

"So the Orientation Stage helps a team get off on the right foot," said Dan.

"That's for sure," said the One Minute Manager. Then he began to smile. "The Orientation Stage reminds me of how dogs behave when they first meet. They run up eagerly but, before they play, they get very cautious and check each other out. I call that the sniffing stage. As the team progresses it will move into other stages."

"I see," laughed Dan, still thinking about the dogs. "Then you're saying that there are several stages and that things change as the team grows."

"That's exactly right. Before we talk about any of the other stages, I'd like you to visit another team in our company that is further along than Ron's team. We have a productivity improvement team that's been meeting for a couple of weeks trying to look at the issue of customer complaints and billing problems. Let me find out when they are having their next meeting and ask them to let you observe."

"Sounds good," said Dan. "I'll call you tomorrow."

"No, I'll find out right now," said the One Minute

Manager as he picked up the phone and called Susan Schaefer. "Susan," he said, "I have a young man up here who wants to learn about high performing teams and I wonder if he could observe the next meeting of your billing task force."

Dan could not hear her, but Susan said, "I suppose he could observe, but he won't learn much about effective teams if he looks at us."

"THAT'S just the point," said the One Minute Manager. "I want him to see how groups grow and develop, and from what you've told me, your team is in the second stage most groups encounter: *Dissatisfaction*, or Stage 2."

"I guess you're right," replied Susan. "We're meeting at 2:00 p.m. on Wednesday. Have him meet me in my office about 1:45 p.m. and I'll brief him."

"Good afternoon," said Dan when he met Susan in the hall outside her office. "The One Minute Manager sent me down here to observe your task force."

"Right," said Susan. "We are having our fourth meeting in a few minutes. The task force has four people from shipping, two from accounting, three from sales and the director of the information services. We're working on improving our billing and accounts receivable process and reducing customer complaints. We're having a hard time pinpointing the problem areas. Why don't you join the meeting but sit a little apart from the others and just observe."

Dan sat in the corner as the others gathered. Susan called the meeting to order about 2:05 p.m. but one of the people said they should wait until everyone was there. Another person left unexpectedly at that point and went down the hall. By 2:10 p.m. everyone was there and Susan opened by saying, "This is our fourth meeting and, although we have set goals of increasing billing accuracy and reducing customer complaints, we haven't agreed upon clear strategies and action plans to accomplish either task."

"That's not true," responded Sam, a member of the sales staff. "We give the accounting department accurate information on our orders but they can't seem to keep track of the information."

Immediately one of the accounting staff and the computer systems director joined in and for a few minutes everyone was talking at once. The session seemed chaotic and Dan soon lost track of what topic was being discussed.

After about five more minutes Susan rapped on the table and said, "Hold it. This isn't getting us anywhere. Everyone is talking at once. I want one person to talk at a time. Let's go around the room and in one sentence I'd like each of you to identify what you think the most important issue is."

The process seemed to help clarify some of the issues. People still seemed frustrated, however, even though it was clear that they were beginning to understand some of the major areas of concern.

"Well, what did you think?" Susan asked Dan as they left the meeting about 3:30 p.m.

"I'm confused," he replied. "That session felt very uncomfortable to me. Everyone seemed frustrated and some people were even angry. When you focused on a task you took control and asked for their input. They seemed to be challenging you and each other or withdrawing from the group. And then you congratulated the team at the end even though you had criticized them earlier."

"I understand your confusion," said Susan. "Let's talk about it more later. I have another appointment right now."

"That session," thought Dan, "reminded me of a lot of the groups I've worked with over the years.

"It's why I don't like groups and meetings. It's why . . .

*

SOME PEOPLE

REFER

TO MEETINGS

AS A PLACE

WHERE

YOU TAKE MINUTES

AND

WASTE HOURS

*

Dan laughed to himself as he thought about that statement. "I guess that's better than saying, 'A camel is a horse designed by a commitee,' although that fits my experience with groups."

Dan was still confused as he went back to the One Minute Manager's office to discuss his experience.

"That was quite a meeting," he said, as he went into the office. "What I'm most confused about is why you called that Stage 2. That group seemed less productive and less friendly than the team you said was at Stage 1."

"That's exactly right," chuckled the One Minute Manager, "and predictable. That's why we call it the *Dissatisfaction* Stage. It's what happens after the honeymoon is over. This card will describe what's going on in this stage."

As the One Minute Manager handed Dan another card, he began to read:

Stage 2—Dissatisfaction

Characteristics
- Discrepancy between expectations and reality
- Confusion and frustration around roles and goals
- Dissatisfaction with dependence on authority
- Expression of dissatisfaction
- Formulation of coalitions
- Feelings of incompetence, confusion, low confidence
- Competition for power, authority and attention
- Low trust
- Some task accomplishment

Needs
- Clarification of big picture
- Redefinition of purpose, roles, goals and structure
- Recommitment to values and norms
- Development of team and task skills
- Development of communication processes including active listening, the exchange of nonjudgmental feedback, conflict management and problem solving
- Valuing of differences
- Access to information and resources
- Encouragement and reassurance
- Recognition of accomplishments
- Open and honest discussion of issues including emotional blocks, coalitions and personality conflicts
- Mutual accountability and responsibility

Issues
- Power
- Control
- Conflict

"Wow," said Dan. "That stage just isn't very effective, is it?"

"Wait a minute," said the One Minute Manager. "You're jumping to conclusions and making a lot of assumptions. I said this was Stage 2, but I didn't say it was an unproductive stage. It's a stage that all teams go through on their way to being productive. It is a stage that is rarely, if ever, avoided."

"You mean to tell me," said Dan, "that all teams have to go through this bad stage or unproductive stage in order to get anywhere?"

"That's right," said the One Minute Manager. "But I wouldn't call it a 'bad' stage any more than I'd call an adolescent a bad person. It's just the process that we have to go through as the team develops. Although this stage is characterized by power struggles and conflict, it also is the seedbed of creativity and valuing differences."

"Well, it seemed to me," said Dan, "that not only was productivity not very high but people were feeling terrible. They weren't liking each other and the morale in the team was low."

"Yes," said the One Minute Manager, "that happens over and over again in teams. There's a dip in morale or commitment as people realize that the team's task is harder than they initially expected. As you read on the card, people get dissatisfied with the team's chairperson or often with each other. They often have negative reactions because the goals seem too high. They may have feelings of confusion or incompetence. As a result of those feelings, morale often takes a dip. In fact, some groups start in this stage. This is especially true when it's an undesirable task like downsizing in an organization. If team members are not there voluntarily or if the committee assignment just feels like extra work, then the group may start with low morale and low productivity, that is, Stage 2. It is important, though, that you remember:

*

NO DEVELOPMENTAL

STAGE

IS BAD

EACH STAGE IS

PART OF THE

JOURNEY

TOWARD

PRODUCTION

*

"Groups need to work through the issues inherent in the Dissatisfaction Stage," continued the One Minute Manager. "They need to be encouraged to express their feelings of frustration and confusion so that those feelings can be dealt with and resolved."

"I'll have to take your word for it," said Dan. "But so much of my experience is similar to what I've just observed that I'm feeling depressed about the possibility of really applying some of your concepts to groups and teams."

" BEFORE we talk more, let's have you observe another team. It might give you some ideas about what might happen next as groups develop."

The shipping department's regular meeting was scheduled for 8:45 a.m. each Monday. Dan awoke early, curious about what the group he would be observing would be like. After a hurried breakfast he got in the car. Then it happened. The car would not start. Despite all his efforts the motor refused to turn over. Time was slipping by. Finally in desperation he called a taxi. By the time he reached the company, the shipping meeting had been in progress for ten minutes. Quietly he slipped in the door and sat in the back of the room. However, his entrance did not go unobserved. All 15 members stopped their work and each member in turn introduced him or herself and welcomed Dan. They wanted him to sit at the round table but Dan refused. Upon completion of the introductions, the group went back to work.

As Dan observed, he noted how enthusiastically they approached the task. They were working on a way to cut the time a certain procedure took by 15 percent. They pointed to the charts and graphs on the walls. Dan was fascinated at their system for tracking progress toward their 15 percent reduction goal and made a promise to explore this process further with the shipping department manager. One thing that puzzled him was: Who was leading the team?

He was totally baffled. The team worked quickly, sharing information and proposing ideas. People differed with each other, even argued, but always seemed to resolve their differences. There was joking and teasing among team members. At one time the team split into three subgroups to come up with a solution to a procedural issue. Then they joined together and reached consensus. The atmosphere was one of high energy and productivity. But who was the leader? There did not seem to be one. The team seemed to move as a unit with different people taking leadership at different times. Dan was puzzled.

At 10:15 a.m. a tall, serious-looking gentleman in his early thirties entered the room.

"Sorry I'm late. I had another commitment," he said.

The team responded with "hellos" and continued its work. The tall gentleman approached Dan.

"Hello. I'm Neil Henry. How are you?"

"Just fine," replied Dan.

"I'll speak with you later. I need to catch up on what's happened here so far in the meeting," said Neil.

Dan was curious about this new delinquent member and how the team would handle a new person. To his surprise, work proceeded at the same pace. Neil contributed ideas, occasionally reinforced and praised, or disagreed. His contributions were no different than others and were accepted in the same way.

At 10:45 a.m. the meeting ended. As they filed out the door, the members expressed pleasure that Dan had been able to join them. Dan was impressed. He had never been to a meeting where so much had been accomplished so smoothly and with such a positive attitude. It was as though the team acted as one unit and not a number of individuals. He couldn't help thinking of the analogy of a well-oiled machine where all parts were functioning in perfect harmony to produce a desired outcome.

His thoughts were interrupted as Neil approached.

"I hope you learned what you wanted," said Neil. "They're quite a team. We've been working together for two years. They really don't need me here anymore."

Dan's eyes widened. "Are you the department head?"

"Why yes," smiled Neil.

Dan stammered a bit. "That's the one thing I couldn't figure out."

"Oh," chuckled Neil. "I know it's different than what you are used to and it wasn't always that way. We've had our rough times. My goal has been to work myself out of a job gradually as the team developed and I'd say we're there, wouldn't you?"

"Absolutely," agreed Dan. "It's all making sense now. You have to change your leadership depending on the stage of development the group is in and the goal is to get the group to the point where they are not only accomplishing the task efficiently but operating effectively as a team."

"You've got it," replied Neil. "When you do that you will have a group in the *Production* Stage."

Following the meeting, Dan hurried to the One Minute Manager's office humming with excitement. "Is he in?" Dan asked.

"Yes, but he has somebody with him. He should be free shortly," smiled Dana, the One Minute Manager's executive assistant.

As he waited, Dan reflected on his experiences over the past few days and jotted down some notes:

1. Members on the performance appraisal committee were enthusiastic, yet concerned about how they fit in. They were in Stage 1: Orientation. They had little knowledge of the task. Ron Tilman provided a lot of direction to clarify the purpose and values, set roles and goals and define tasks. There was little two-way interaction except at the end when he asked how people were feeling and if they understood the time lines and next steps.

2. Susan Schaefer's productivity team members were confused and disgruntled. They were in Stage 2: Dissatisfaction. They were making headway but it was slow. Sue was very assertive in the management of the group, but she also encouraged people to express their thoughts and opinions.

3. The shipping department was operating so smoothly and with such efficiency that the absence of Neil, the department head, seemed to have little impact. He said they were in the production stage. The team was enthusiastic and highly productive. Neil's contributions were no different from any other member's, but how did that group get there?

Dan pondered this question. Instinctively, he knew there was a piece missing. A team could not just move from a disgruntled group of individuals into such a synergistic, productive unit.

As he thought, the One Minute Manager appeared. "Hello, Dan, how's it going?"

Dan's excitement had now given way to a frown.

"You look puzzled," responded the One Minute Manager.

"Well, I am," said Dan. "You see, I witnessed a team getting started. The team leader was careful to lay out all the groundwork and provide direction. The next group I observed was moving slowly, accomplishing the task, but seemed to be very fragmented. More like the meetings I'm used to. Susan did not appear disturbed by this. She provided a lot of direction, both in terms of tasks and getting people to work together, and she listened patiently and encouraged people."

"Next I visited Neil's team. They were in the production stage. They seemed to have it all together. They were enjoying each other and the work and the group was managing itself. My question is: How did they get there? Did I miss something?"

"That you did," smiled the One Minute Manager. "You leap-frogged over an important stage in team development. You went straight from dissatisfaction to production. Before I talk about the missing stage, let me give you a summary card for Stage 4: Production." It read:

Stage 4—Production

Characteristics
- Clear purpose, values, roles and goals
- Empowering team practices that free team energy and lead to continuous improvement
- Relationships and communication built on trust, mutual respect and openness
- Flexibility and shared leadership that allow the team to respond to new challenges
- Optimal productivity and high standards
- Recognition and appreciation for individual and team accomplishments
- High morale

Needs
- Continued focus on productivity
- New challenges
- Recognition and celebration of team accomplishments
- Individual acknowledgment
- Decision-making autonomy within boundaries

Issues
- New challenges
- Continued growth and learning

"THE characteristics described there certainly describe how Neil's team operated," said Dan. "Tell me about the stage I missed."

"That stage is called *Integration*. It's the bridge between the dissatisfaction you witnessed in Susan's team and the efficiency and excitement in Neil's."

"What happens in that stage?" questioned Dan.

"The best way to understand the integration stage is to . . ."

"Experience it," jumped in Dan.

"Right on," said the One Minute Manager.

"Let me see. This stage is often fairly brief," thought the One Minute Manager.

Suddenly the intercom on the One Minute Manager's desk came alive. "Louise Gilmore is on the line. Should I have her call later?"

"Wait a moment," replied the One Minute Manager. "I'll take it now." Turning to Dan with a smile, he said, "Excuse the interruption, Dan, but this may be exactly what we are looking for."

"Hello, Louise. What can I do you for?"

After a long silence, the One Minute Manager smiled broadly. "That's wonderful, Louise. As I've said, you have to trust the process. It works. By the way, how would you feel about a visitor in your meeting tomorrow morning? He is a friend of mine who is interested in how groups develop and it sounds like your meeting would fill a missing gap. Thanks. He will be there."

"It's all set. Tomorrow you will attend a strategic planning meeting that Louise is running—that is, if you'd care to."

"Of course," Dan responded eagerly.

The next morning Dan arrived early at the office. He had spent the cab ride thinking of how fortunate he was to have met such a special person who seemed to get real pleasure in sharing information with others. Information is power and the One Minute Manager gave it freely.

Louise Gilmore, the vice president of strategic planning, was sitting quietly at her desk when Dan arrived. She seemed to come alive when he walked in and with a big smile and firm handshake greeted him warmly. Dan was struck by her vitality and friendliness.

Together they entered the meeting room where the six group members were chatting and joking amicably.

Louise introduced Dan as he found a seat. All team members greeted him cordially but with a bit of reserve. Dan couldn't help feeling that his presence made them a bit uncomfortable.

The meeting began with Louise reviewing the struggle the team had had in determining next year's direction and goals and then the outcomes they had finally agreed upon. There was much joking and laughing during the review and friendly kidding of one another. It seemed that they enjoyed and valued each other's company in spite of or because of the prior disagreements Louise had mentioned. Louise laughed along with them.

Today's agenda began with new decisions to be made. The group engaged immediately, listening to one another, building on each other's ideas and often agreeing readily. Dan watched in fascination at how smoothly things were proceeding. After opening the meeting, Louise gave control of the meeting to other members as the topics of discussion changed.

There was an air of respect and politeness in the group. Dan noticed some members became less vocal as time went on. Much to his surprise, just as Dan assumed a decision was made, Louise spoke up.

"Bill, you haven't said anything for the past ten minutes. Are you having some reservations?"

"Well, yes, but they are minor," replied Bill.

"Please share them," said Louise. "If you remember, our best, most creative decisions have come from our disagreements."

"OK," replied Bill and he proceeded cautiously. At first the others protested and then the group began a heated discussion of the pros and cons of the new points Bill had made.

Dan thought to himself, "Uh, oh, she's lost it. The team had been working well before this."

Louise listened, facilitated disagreements, built on the merits of each position and added her own. Others began to do likewise.

Somewhat tentatively Bill spoke up again. "Building on the plans on which we've agreed, if our expected profit in new products is solid and the cuts we're making in other departments are adequate, we could afford to invest in needed capital improvements."

As he spoke, others listened and heads began to nod. Bill then asked if there was a consensus on the decision. All team members responded enthusiastically. Shortly after, the meeting adjourned. There was a feeling of accomplishment and eagerness in the air.

The team members sauntered out, each stopping to shake hands with Dan. Team members seemed to feel confident and productive. Dan heard comments like: "Good meeting." "Glad you could join us," and, "We got through that one."

When the room emptied, Louise and the One Minute Manager joined him. "Well Dan, what did you think?"

"Amazing," replied Dan. "I thought the group had blown it for a while, but individuals seemed to feel better and more confident after they had disagreed. Also, I noticed you opened the meeting, then let them manage it, but you jumped back in and helped them out as necessary."

"You've got it," smiled Louise. "People are feeling good because they have worked through some struggles together. It's like in a new marriage when neither spouse wants to disagree even when they don't agree. Later after they work through some differences, their marriage can be stronger. The danger to a team occurs when this euphoric feeling prevents a loss of productivity that comes from disagreement. The result can be a tendency toward Groupthink."

"Groupthink, what's that?" interrupted Dan.

"A famous psychologist coined that term," replied the One Minute Manager, "while studying some groups that were advising the presidents of the United States. Irving Janis discovered that, often, social pressure prevented members from disagreeing."

"Oh, so Groupthink occurs when group members are afraid to disagree so they don't say anything at all," responded Dan thoughtfully. "No one is willing to rock the boat."

"Exactly. My role at this point is to encourage disagreement and to help the team work through the conflict. I'm concerned about the team developing the confidence to manage disagreement and to value differences. These are all important activities in the *Integration* Stage—the stage this group is in."

"In addition, the team was beginning to manage itself. If I continue to be in there directing, however, that would never happen. My role at this stage is to support their efforts at self-management and to model effective membership."

"But what if they really get into trouble?" questioned Dan.

"Rest assured, I'd be there," replied Louise with a smile.

"I'm sure you would," said Dan. "And thank you. You've helped me a lot."

"Don't mention it," said Louise as she handed Dan a card. 'You-know-who' wanted me to give you this card which describes Stage 3: Integration."

Stage 3—Integration

Characteristics
- Increased clarity and commitment on roles, goals, tasks and structure
- Increased commitment to norms and values
- Increased task accomplishment—moderate to high
- Growing trust, cohesion, harmony and mutual respect
- Willingness to share responsibility, leadership and control
- Understanding and valuing of differences
- Use of team language—"we" rather than "me"
- Tendency to avoid conflict

Needs
- Integration of team and individual roles and goals, norms and structure
- Continued skill development
- Encouragement to share different perspectives and to disagree in order to further develop problem-solving skills
- Continued building of trust and positive relationships
- Shared responsibility for leadership and team functioning
- A focus on increasing productivity
- Evaluation of and learning from each experience
- Recognition and celebration of success

Issues
- Sharing of control
- Avoidance of conflict

"WHAT are the big-picture learnings from your visits to some of our work teams?" asked the One Minute Manager as Dan Brockway entered his office.

"First of all, there are four different stages of group development that a team can be in at any one moment in time," said Dan. "The first stage for most teams is *orientation* where *productivity* is *low* because team members are not clear on goals and tasks and have minimal knowledge and skills about how to function as a team. *Morale* is *high*, though, as everyone is excited about being a part of the team and has high expectations.

At the other extreme is *production* where the team is humming. *Productivity* is *high* as team members have the knowledge, skills and *morale* to be a *high*-performing team. In between those two extremes are two stages: *dissatisfaction*, when the honeymoon is over and the initial high expectations of the team are seen as being more difficult to achieve; and *integration*, when the team is learning to work together resolving differences and developing confidence and cohesion."

"Good summary," said the One Minute Manager. "Any other learnings?"

"I noticed that productivity increased slowly through the four stages," said Dan. "It started low in orientation, and continued to improve through dissatisfaction and integration until it was high in production. On the other hand, morale or enthusiasm started high in orientation and then took a dip in dissatisfaction, but then it began to increase again in integration and production."

"I'm impressed that you noticed that," said the One Minute Manager. "One group development theorist has put those dimensions on a chart that shows how morale and productivity vary during each stage. It looks something like this," he said as he drew the chart on the flipchart.

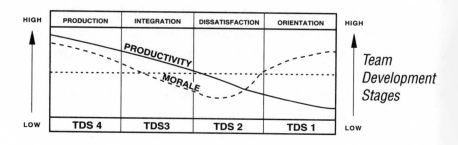

"The TDS stands for Team Development Stage. Notice how the productivity and morale dimensions change," said the One Minute Manager.

"That's very helpful," said Dan. "It makes it seem very clear."

"Pictures are often worth a thousand words. Any other insights?"

"Yes," said Dan. "It seems each stage needs a different type of leadership. Here's where I want more information. How does a team leader know the very best way to work with a team during each stage?"

"IT sounds like you have mastered diagnosis and now you are ready to learn adaptability—when to use what leadership style. That requires that you become a *Situational Leader*," smiled the One Minute Manager.

"A what?"

"A Situational Leader," repeated the One Minute Manager. "For a long time it was thought that there were only two ways to manage a team of people: autocratically or democratically. With autocratic leadership the emphasis was on telling your people what to do, how to do it, where to do it, and when to do it. Team performance was paramount. With democratic leadership the emphasis was on listening to your people, praising their efforts and facilitating their interactions with each other. Team morale was deemed to be the best way to maximize the group's performance. There were two problems with these two extremes of leadership."

"I bet one of them was the either/or way of looking at things," interjected Dan. "That always leads to an 'I'm right, you're wrong' way of looking at the world."

"Precisely," said the One Minute Manager. "As a result, we would have great pendulum swings in terms of managing groups or teams. If you were too autocratic, people would complain after a while and say: 'You're too tough. You're stifling creativity,' and, 'You're controlling everything.' Then, feeling bad, the leader would shift over to the other extreme and involve everyone in decision making with a more democratic and participative leadership style."

"But that could be overused as well, right?" asked Dan.

"Absolutely," said the One Minute Manager. "And then pretty soon everyone would be complaining that people are feeling good but nothing is getting done. There is too much socializing, or meetings are taking too long."

"And pretty soon there would be another drastic shift to the other extreme," laughed Dan. "A real yo-yo. I've certainly seen that."

"You've got it," said the One Minute Manager. "What I like about Situational Leadership® II that it eliminates that flip-flop approach while, at the same time, recognizes that there are two behaviors involved in leadership: providing direction or autocratic behavior, and providing support or democratic behavior." With that, the One Minute Manager began to draw a large square and divide it into four equal boxes. When he finished labeling the boxes, he handed it to Dan:

The Four Leadership Styles
of Situational Leadership® II
in a Group or Team Context

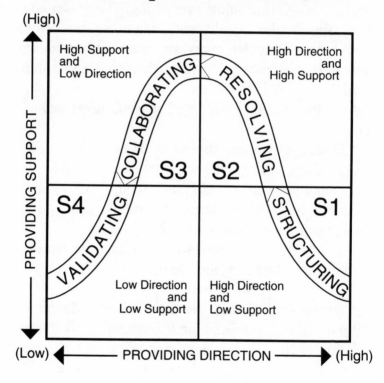

As you can see from the Situational Leadership® II Model," continued the One Minute Manager when Dan looked up from examining the drawing, "there are four combinations of direction and support. When applied to one-on-one leadership situations, the four styles had been called directing (S1), coaching (S2), supporting (S3), and delegating (S4). When it came to applying these concepts to group leadership, as we're doing here, it was felt that those labels needed to be modified to more directly reflect what groups needed at each stage of the team development.

I used to be a school teacher when I first got out of college," continued the One Minute Manager. "There were two different approaches to teaching depending on your assumptions about kids. One approach assumed that kids come to class with their barrels empty of knowledge and experience. If that was the case, what would be the job of the teacher?"

"To fill up their barrels with knowledge," smiled Dan.

"Exactly," said the One Minute Manager. "To me, providing direction is a barrel-filling behavior. That's exactly what is needed when a team is in the orientation stage of development. People are confused about roles and goals and there is a high need for information, skills and structure. The reason a lot of support is not needed in this stage is that team members are already enthusiastic and committed."

"That's the style that Ron Tilman used with his new task force and it seemed appropriate."

"It was," said the One Minute Manager. "If Ron had started with being participative and supportive, it would have been inappropriate because the task force came to its first meeting needing information and direction. Their barrels were *empty*."

"When is it more important to provide support then?" asked Dan.

"When the team already has experience and skills working together but for some reason has become bogged down. In our teaching analogy, the second approach assumed that students bring to class a *'full barrel'* of knowledge and experience but it is not particularly organized. Therefore, it's the job of the teacher to draw that knowledge and experience out of the kids and then help them organize it. Providing support is a "barrel drawing-out" activity. The leader listens, supports, and facilitates the team's interactions in a collaborating style."

"That's what Louise Gilmore did with the strategic planning committee," said Dan. "She drew almost everything from the group."

"That was appropriate for that committee," said the One Minute Manager. "They had moved past the Dissatisfaction Stage and were learning to work with each other. They didn't need a lot of direction because they had developed the skills necessary to function as a team and had resolved some of the issues of the Dissatisfaction Stage."

"How do the skills of resolving and validating fit into this?"

"Resolving is high on both providing direction and providing support and validating is low on both behaviors," said the One Minute Manager.

"Is resolving, then, a 'barrel-filling' and 'barrel drawing-out' activity?"

"Yes, indeed," said the One Minute Manager. "It involves providing both direction and support, telling and listening."

"Susan Schaefer used that style with her productivity improvement group. Since they were dissatisfied, morale was dropping and they needed to express their opinions and they needed support from her."

"But since they were still developing skills as a team," said the One Minute Manager, "they also required direction."

"With a validating style like Neil used with the shipping department," said Dan, "neither 'barrel filling' nor 'barrel drawing-out' is needed because the group's barrel is not only filled, but it is organized."

"You have that right," said the One Minute Manager. "Now you can see why adaptability is important."

Dan leaned back in a reflective way and said, "It seems like . . .

*

EFFECTIVE

LEADERS

ADJUST THEIR STYLE

TO PROVIDE

WHAT THE GROUP

CAN'T PROVIDE

FOR ITSELF

*

"THAT'S a good way to put it," said the One Minute Manager. "For any group to be effective, someone has to be attending to both task functions and maintenance functions. The question is whether it has to be the designated group leader or not."

"Task functions?" wondered Dan.

"*Task functions* are behaviors which focus on getting the job done," said the One Minute Manager. "They focus on what the group is supposed to be doing. Task functions include activities such as setting the agenda, establishing goals, giving direction, initiating discussion, setting time limits, giving and seeking information and summarizing."

"So task functions are related to directive behavior," said Dan. "What are maintenance functions?"

"Group *maintenance functions* focus on developing and maintaining the group's harmony and cohesiveness. Such activities focus on how the group is functioning. They include recognition, listening, encouraging participation, conflict management and relationship building."

"Those are all supportive behaviors?"

"They sure are," said the One Minute Manager. "What you need to learn, and Situational Leadership® II certainly helps, is that, although these functions need to be fulfilled for a team to be effective, filling them is not necessarily the job of the manager or designated team leader. In fact, as team members are able to take over these functions, it is best for the manager to move out of those roles."

"So there is a smooth transition of leadership style and functions as the team progresses," said Dan.

"That's exactly right," said the One Minute Manager.

"In the Orientation Stage, team members bring enthusiasm and commitment to meetings, but little knowledge, so they need direction (Structuring-S1). In the Dissatisfaction Stage, team members are not high on either competence or commitment. They are struggling with the task as well as how to work together so they need both direction and support (Resolving-S2). In the Integration Stage, team members have the skills to perform well but still need to build their confidence or morale so they need support and encouragement (Collaborating-S3). And finally, when a team reaches the Production Stage they have high skills and morale so the leader can stand aside or join in and let them work with minimal interference (Validating-S4)."

"So in the Orientation Stage, task functions are the main concern for the leader," said Dan. "While in the Dissatisfaction Stage, the team is not able to handle either task or maintenance concerns. As a result, the burden for both often falls on the leader. In the Integration Stage, the team is managing the task concerns but needs help on team maintenance. Then, finally, in the Production Stage both task and maintenance functions are being attended to by team members.

"IT sounds as if you have a good grasp of those concepts," said the One Minute Manager.

"Yes," said Dan, "I'm excited about how all this fits together and I can't wait to get back to Maria Sanchez and tell her what I've learned."

"That's a good idea," said the One Minute Manager. "I find that one of the best ways to test my own understanding is to try to teach someone else."

"Great," said Dan. "I think I'll call her as soon as I get back to the office and arrange a lunch meeting."

"Listen," said the One Minute Manager, "I'd like to meet Maria. Would you mind if I joined you and sat back while you share those ideas?"

"That would be perfect," Dan replied. "It would be a good check for me and since you've convinced me how perceptive Maria is, she might come up with some questions I haven't thought of. Let's call her right now and set the time."

That Friday, Dan, Maria and the One Minute Manager met for lunch. After ordering their meal, Dan pulled out a folder from his briefcase and began.

"Maria," he said, "that letter you wrote about teamwork was really unsettling to me so I called my friend, the One Minute Manager, for some help. I wanted some advice about how to convince you that what we were teaching was right. To my surprise, he agreed with your comments about the importance of working in groups. He's been showing me how working in groups differs from managing one-on-one. I've been spending some time observing teams in action and talking with the One Minute Manager concerning his ideas about team development and leadership. I wanted to share with you what I've learned, so I put this Situational Leadership® II diagram together that, I think, summarizes how a leader can best work with and develop a group into a high performing team." Dan pulled the diagram out of his folder and explained the stages of group development, told Maria how each called for different leadership behaviors and described the changes in productivity and morale that occurred over time.

Group/Team Development and Situational Leadership® II

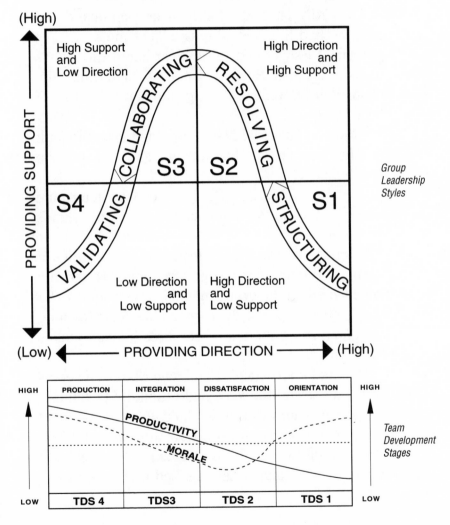

MARIA listened attentively as Dan talked and after he had finished, she said, "Let me see if I've got this. First, I need to be clear about the team's goals and tasks. Second, I need to determine the stage of development of the group in relation to that task."

"Right so far," said Dan, "and don't forget to look at the morale of the group as well as the productivity."

"Yes," said Maria. "Third, I need to determine which style fits the stage of the team's development."

"Right," said Dan. "Each leadership style varies in terms of the amount of direction, support and the involvement of the group in making decisions. In S1 the leader is primarily responsible for providing direction. In S4 the team sets direction and makes decisions."

"I think I understand, Dan," said Maria. "It seems clear and straightforward and I think it fits some of the groups I am working with. I'd like to try some of your thoughts out and see how they work for me. Do you think we could meet again in two weeks to discuss these ideas after I've had a chance to use them?"

At that, the One Minute Manager jumped in and said, "I think that's an excellent idea. After you have tested the ideas, you may have some additional thoughts and questions. I would look forward to that discussion."

"I would too," said Dan. "Maria, I'm glad you wrote that letter. I certainly have learned a lot from all this and I'm going to do some more thinking also. Let's all get together the week after next, same time, same place."

During the next two weeks Maria focused primarily on two teams. The first was a quality task force that had just recently been convened and it was easy to diagnose that they were in the Orientation Stage. They were not clear about goals and hadn't yet defined their individual roles or an action plan. Maria decided to focus the group's energy on understanding goals, establishing roles and defining the skills needed and the necessary first steps. The meeting went well and Maria felt good about the progress made.

The other group was Maria's own work unit. It was harder for her to diagnose the stage this group was in. They seemed to like, enjoy and support each other, but there was an underlying uneasiness and some tension between some of the members of the group. She couldn't decide whether they were in the Dissatisfaction or Integration Stage and so she had more difficulty in deciding what leadership style would work best. Maria wasn't sure if her close connection with her group might be distorting her views. As she reflected on her work in preparation for the meeting with Dan and the One Minute Manager, she jotted down several questions in her notebook:

1. Can a team move from Orientation to Production without the help of a team leader?
2. Once I determine a team's developmental stage and have decided on a leadership style, how long should I stay with that leadership style?
3. Can a manager's involvement with the unit get in the way of her ability to diagnose its stage of development?

WHEN Maria, Dan and the One Minute Manager got together, Maria immediately spoke up. "I'm glad to see you both," she said. "I've had some success with using the model but it has raised some questions for me as well. I've written my questions down on this sheet of paper." Dan and the One Minute Manager read over the list. "These are very important concerns," said the One Minute Manager. "I think we should take them in order."

"Wait a minute," said Dan, "I'd like to add one other question to the list. One of the units in my plant has been functioning beautifully for six months, but last week when I was there they seemed to be very tentative in their behavior, reluctant to speak out, and I felt some unspoken tension. It didn't seem like the same team I'd met with last month so my question is: 'Do teams ever regress to a previous developmental stage? If so, why, and what can be done to prevent it?' "

"That's quite a set of questions," said the One Minute Manager. "Let's finish our lunch and go over to the office. I think we could work better with a flipchart and room to spread out our work."

Back in the office as Maria put the four questions on a flipchart, the One Minute Manager got a poster from his conference room and taped it on the wall.

*

THE MOST IMPORTANT

FUNCTION

OF A LEADER

IS TO HELP

THE GROUP

MOVE THROUGH THE

STAGES OF DEVELOPMENT

*

THE One Minute Manager explained, "I put this statement up because I think it relates to your first question, Maria."

"I take it from that," Maria said, "that diagnosing the stage of development and being adaptable enough to deliver the appropriate leadership style are the first two skills, but they are just the beginning. My primary job is to continue to change my style whenever possible to help the group move through the stages to Stage 4 where they will be a high-performing team."

"That's it," replied the One Minute Manager. "Now we're talking about the third skill—empowerment— that an effective team leader needs to develop besides diagnosis and adaptability. Empowerment involves gradually turning over the responsibility for direction and support to the team. In many groups today empowerment starts at the first meeting when they do not have a former leader. When that does occur, the organization has to provide the group with help during the chartering process so the group can stay on a course that is helpful to the organization. So empowerment involves managing the journey from dependence on a leader or some outside sponsor to interdependence, from external control to internal control. I can illustrate this best by referring back to the four basic Situational Leadership® II styles." With that, the One Minute Manager quickly drew the model on a second flipchart he had in front of the room.

The Four Leadership Styles of Situational Leadership® II in a Group or Team Context

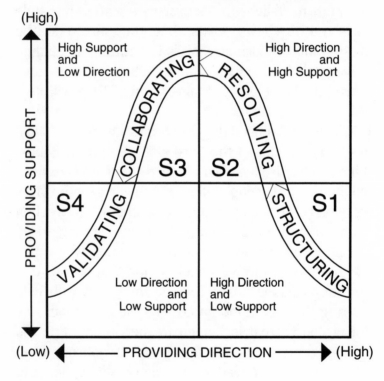

"Imagine the curve going through the leadership styles is a railroad track. If you want to get from Style 1 to Style 4, what two stations do you have to stop at along the way?"

"Style 2—Resolving, and Style 3—Collaborating," said Dan. "If that's true, then I would assume it's not possible to skip a stage. In other words, you couldn't go right from Orientation to Production."

"Except for some groups that might start in Stage 2 as we discussed earlier, groups generally do not skip stages. No matter how sophisticated team members are about the task or how experienced they are in group dynamics, they still have to create a team and the process of developing a high performing team requires going through those states. That also means that your leadership style has to follow this same track—you can't skip a style."

"That's really interesting," said Maria. "In retrospect I can remember several times when I've started off using a collaborating (S3), participative style with a new group, particularly when the group was set up as a quality circle or employee problem-solving group."

"How did it work?"

"Horribly," said Maria. "I drove them immediately into dissatisfaction. Then, not knowing what I was doing, I would get angry and move straight from a supporting Style 3 to a directing Style 1. And that really made the group more angry and more unhappy."

"My rule of thumb," said the One Minute Manager," is when in doubt, whether it be a new group or an already established group, start with a more directive style because if you have misdiagnosed and the team is farther along in its developmental stage than you thought, it is much easier to loosen up than tighten up. But if you assume a team is further along than it is and you start off too participative and supportive and you have to back up and be more directive, members will resent it, even if it is appropriate."

"So you're saying people in general resent tightening up on leadership style," said Maria.

"Absolutely," said the One Minute Manager. "I used to tell my wife when she was a teacher not to smile too much until November. If she started off as Ms. Human Relations and wanted to be the kids' friend right away and they did not perform, it would be murder to retain control."

"I think I buy this managing the journey role for team leaders and recognize the importance of staying on the railroad tracks," said Maria. "But I could use some help on my second question—how long should you stay at each station?"

"REMEMBER our discussion a couple of weeks ago," said the One Minute Manager, "when we said that a structuring style is for the Orientation Stage. It's a start-up style and should be used to build the team charter, share necessary information, explain initial goals and tasks and help the team develop the skills necessary to become more effective. If a leader stays in a highly directive style for long, however, team members will soon feel resentment about being told over and over what to do and how to do it. They will be less inclined to contribute their ideas and opinions. Productivity, satisfaction and creativity will all suffer as a result."

"That makes a lot of sense to me," said Maria. "I know that whenever I have been in that kind of a group situation I don't feel I have much personal influence and thus soon lose interest."

"That's right," said the One Minute Manager. "And that's why it's important to move very quickly to a resolving style and to begin to encourage members to share their ideas and opinions. People begin to feel empowered when their ideas are valued. Remember, a group can have process goals such as open communication and shared leadership as well as task goals. Stating those goals is often a good way to move to a resolving style and to encourage input from team members."

"Good idea," said Maria. "But why do groups move into a stage of dissatisfaction if the leadership behavior has shifted to resolving at an appropriate time?"

"That's a good question," said the One Minute Manager. "It would be nice to avoid that dissatisfaction stage and move to being a high performing team. Appropriate leadership behavior at the right time can certainly reduce the amount of dissatisfaction, but it will never eliminate it. As people begin to express their opinions and state their needs, differences will emerge. As a result, some members get competitive with one another and engage in power struggles, others withdraw and still others get discouraged and frustrated with the difficulty of the task. The reality of the hard work sets in after the honeymoon is over. The team is struggling during the Dissatisfaction Stage for a sense of purpose and independence. It's a time of turbulence."

"Yes. It sounds like something to avoid if possible," said Maria.

"Not so!" said the One Minute Manager. "It's a creative and dynamic stage as well. As I mentioned to Dan, it is the adolescent stage in a team's life. The team has to go through this awkward period before it can move to adulthood and the Production Stage. Unfortunately, lots of groups get stuck in this stage and that's what leads to the negative feelings about groups that is so common. I have found that just knowing that this stage is inevitable helps me keep my commitment to persevere and to progress to the next stage."

"What is needed at this point," continued the One Minute Manager, "is to gradually reduce the amount of direction and to increase the encouragement and support the manager gives. Morale is declining and so we need to find ways to catch the team doing things right as well as to continue to help build skills and knowledge. The team needs to learn how to manage their communication and decision making. It needs to develop ground rules for listening and managing conflict and encouraging everyone's input. Remember, we need to try to provide the kind of behavior that the team is not able to provide for itself."

Dan jumped in at this point and said, "What you just said turned on a light for me. You don't just jump from a structuring to a resolving style. You gradually reduce the amount of direction or task behavior and increase the amount of support or process behavior as you progress through each stage."

"You've got it," said the One Minute Manager. "It's a step-by-step process. Don't forget, in addition to increasing support and reducing direction you're also increasing team involvement in the decision making process. This by itself is a supportive behavior, an empowering behavior. Team responsibility for both the task and the process is increasing and consequently the team should become less dependent on the formal leader."

"What happens if this process continues?" asked Dan. "Does the team leader work himself right out of a job?"

"Well, not quite," said the One Minute Manager. "There's always a role for a team leader, but it doesn't mean maintaining control or keeping the team dependent upon the leader. In fact:

*

YOU WILL

NEVER, NEVER, NEVER

HAVE

AN EMPOWERED,

SELF-DIRECTED TEAM

UNLESS THE LEADER

IS WILLING

TO SHARE CONTROL

*

"If we're interested in productivity and human satisfaction," continued the One Minute Manager, "it is important that everyone involved be empowered to influence the decisions that affect them."

"It may go beyond productivity and satisfaction," said Maria thoughtfully. "I read an article the other day that suggests that people who are involved in decisions at work actually live longer than those who are not."

"Interesting," said the One Minute Manager, "and it makes sense. I know that the most devastating situations in my career are those times when I have no say in important decisions that affect me at work."

"Well, getting back to group development and changing leadership behavior," said Maria, "the leader has to gradually give up control in order for the team to become successful and self-directed."

"Not quite give it up," said the One Minute Manager, "but rather be willing to share it. When that happens the leader is no longer making decisions for the team, but rather participating in these decisions. The team with the leader as a member is now a self-directed team."

"That's a tough shift for a lot of us," said Dan, "because as a manager I've been taught that making decisions and maintaining control is my job."

"I know," said the One Minute Manager, "and what I am suggesting is that your job as a manager is to help people and teams develop so they have competence and commitment and the ability to share in making decisions. Remember, a high performing team is more creative and better at problem solving than any individual functioning alone."

"**I** THINK you have answered my first two questions about the role of the team leader and how long one should stay in a particular leadership style," said Maria. "It would seem to me to be more appropriate to discuss Dan's question around regression before we move to my concerns about diagnosis and involvement."

"Sounds fine to me," said the One Minute Manager. "Fire away, Dan."

"Once teams are in the Production Stage, do they ever regress?" asked Dan.

"Yes, they do," replied the One Minute Manager. "When teams gain, lose or change members, when the task changes or if a major event occurs which disrupts group functioning, the group will move back to Stage 3 and even into Stage 2. You can expect it."

"As a leader, then, you need to move your leadership to match the stage," said Dan.

"Right you are," said the One Minute Manager. "When you are dealing with a high performing team and you are delegating, if a problem occurs, you can't go from Validating (Style 4), back to Structuring (Style 1). That would be the ultimate derailment. You have to back track to Collaborating (Style 3) and try to find out what's going wrong. Then you determine whether you need to move back to Resolving (Style 2) and either redirect or reprimand to get the group back to proper functioning."

"So when a setback occurs," said Dan, "you're suggesting I need to keep on the railroad tracks and move back one leadership style at a time until I can get the group to deal with the problem."

"You've got it," said the One Minute Manager. "Just be careful not to get derailed by jumping the track and skipping a style forward to reinforce growth in group development or backward to handle a regression.

"That's helpful," said Dan. "I think I need to hear that over and over again. Let's go to Maria's last question. Can a manager get so involved that he or she can't decide what stage a group is in? I'm particularly interested in that question because it involves the team leader's role of participant observer."

"What?" wondered Maria.

"Before I began observing some of the work groups in the One Minute Manager's company he told me that an effective team leader, or team member for that matter, had to be fully engaged in the *content* or agenda—what the group was working on—and yet be able to step back and observe the *process* or dynamics which are occuring.

"That's exactly what I'm talking about," said Maria. "Sometimes I felt I was so emotionally involved in the decision itself, it was hard to be aware of how the decision was being made and therefore what stage of development the group was in."

"When I was observing your groups," said Dan, turning to the One Minute Manager, "I didn't have that problem because I wasn't actually a member of the group. I was just a *process observer.*"

"Good point," said the One Minute Manager. "One strategy I often use to minimize the impact my involvement may have on the clarity of my observation is to assign a group member to be the process observer for the group and report periodically on what he or she has observed about communication, decision making, conflict management or other areas of concern. While that member is playing that role, he or she cannot get involved in the content of the discussion."

"Why not?" asked Maria.

"It helps in the beginning when members are learning observation skills to separate out the two roles. However, if at any time in the discussion the process observer feels strongly about what is being discussed, that person can ask to be relieved of the process role so he or she can get involved in the content. Someone else will then step out and assume the role."

"That sounds interesting," said Maria. "So you rotate the process consultant role."

"Yes," said the One Minute Manager. "This helps teach the skills of process observation to all of the group members and raises the awareness of the group about how it is functioning."

"Then if there is a problem or we get stuck, we can use the process information to help us understand what the problems are so we can do something about them. Being fully aware of our own behavior helps move the group through its developmental stages."

"Could you explain that in more detail?" Maria interjected.

"I had a group one time in the Dissatisfaction Stage. I was so embroiled in it, I was helpless. I knew we were in trouble, but I didn't know why or what to do about it. I couldn't tell if we were in Stage 1 or 2," said the One Minute Manager.

"Shouldn't that difference have been clear?" asked Maria somewhat surprised.

"No, not really. Energy was very high and tension was obvious. However questions were about roles and goals and strategies which I thought were orientation needs. Nothing fit neatly."

"Go on," said Maria.

"Well, on a whim, you see I was very new at this, I asked one group member to sit outside the group for one hour and observe how we were communicating. I provided her with a list of questions to serve as a guide like: Who talks? Who talks to whom? Who follows whom? At the end of the hour she reported back. Much to our dismay she counted forty times in that one hour when we interrupted one another."

"Just that one piece of information helped us identify a real problem characteristic of the Dissatisfaction Stage and correct it. All group members monitored their own interactions and we made great strides toward resolution," continued the One Minute Manager.

"I see," said Maria. "You could also give the list to all members to fill out periodically during a meeting to monitor your progress, couldn't you?"

"Yes. A strategy such as that promotes both awareness and mutual responsibility to monitor group functioning," smiled the One Minute Manager.

"How about using a third party to sit in your meeting and monitor group process?" asked Dan, who had been sitting quietly. "That way you wouldn't have to pull a member out or take meeting time to focus on process issues."

"THAT is also a strategy and a useful one, especially if the group is stuck. Sometimes a third, uninvolved party can give straight objective feedback which a member could not do. It could be just the stimulation the group needs. In those cases the process observer acts as an objective candid camera which removes any question of vested interest," said the One Minute Manager.

"I can see how that could be very helpful in the Dissatisfaction Stage or whenever you want objective help with team building from an outside source," agreed Maria.

"Yes. It can be very helpful to the group," said the One Minute Manager, "but I wouldn't depend on it as a steady diet. Remember, the important thing is to transfer the skills of participant observation to the group. Group members need to assume the responsibility of their own monitoring or they will never become a high performing team. Your job as a one minute manager is to *empower* them."

"I can see how that is essential," said Dan. "Groups are so complex there is no way I could stay on top of all that's going on myself."

THE One Minute Manager sat back quietly for a moment. A pensive look came over his face. Then he spoke. "Years ago my mentor taught me a powerful lesson about empowerment. One day I was complaining about how overloaded I felt. I was responsible for all that went on in my department and couldn't keep up. He listened patiently while I ranted and raved and then said simply, 'You're missing the point. Your job is to educate your people, to help them develop to the point where they can take responsibility for their work and to give them opportunities to perform.' I was taken aback. Seeing this, he went on to explain:

*

THE WORDS

"LEADER"

AND

"EDUCATOR"

ARE SYNONYMOUS

*

"Don't you mean trainer rather than educator?" asked Dan.

"No," said the One Minute Manager. "You have to remember that we train animals but we educate people. As a leader you are a teacher. Your primary job is to develop your people. You can't depend on seminars or training sessions to do that for you. In every group there is a well of creativity and talent. Your job is to help all team members develop the skills and knowledge so they become self-directed *and* to provide an environment where they feel willing to risk, to grow, to take responsibility and to use their creativity. Unless you do this, you will constantly feel behind the eight ball and what's worse, you will never be involved with self-directed teams. It's a self-fulfilling prophecy. If you believe groups can be high performing and you help them develop the appropriate skills and knowledge and the freedom to act, teams will respond both creatively and responsibly. That will make your life a whole lot easier."

"So empowering means helping teams develop their skills and knowledge and supporting them to use their talents," replied Maria.

"That's right," agreed the One Minute Manager. "An important thing to remember is that to be fully contributing, individuals and groups have to feel free to do so. In fact, they have to know that you want them to win. When they know that, teams will strive to be the best. They will set stretching goals, assume responsibility and take risks. Even critical feedback will be accepted if teams see it as part of their developmental process and if it is focused on helping them win."

"That's powerful stuff," exclaimed Maria.

"That's empowerment," smiled the One Minute Manager. "Teams feel empowered when they are involved, contributing and productive."

"Well I've felt involved, contributing and productive working with you both," said Dan. "This has been a very important meeting for me. Both of you have been so helpful."

"Learning from each other is what it's all about," replied the One Minute Manager, checking his watch. "Real empowerment comes from sharing. I don't mean just with each other, but with members on every team. I have a board meeting in half an hour so I'll need to move along. It's been a pleasure meeting with you, Maria, and thank you for your letter that started the ball rolling. If I can be of further assistance, call me anytime. Good luck."

"Thanks," said Maria. "I will. I'm going to use my own work unit as a focus for these concepts."

"I'm anxious to continue to use what I've learned, too," said Dan.

ALMOST immediately both Dan and Maria began applying what they had learned from the One Minute Manager about team leadership. In fact, Dan integrated the concepts in the Essentials of Management course he was teaching.

He taught the managers in the program that the steps to empowering others begin with *diagnosis.* In determining the stage of development he suggested that they might use the characteristics of high performing teams as an initial comparison. Everyone learned to use the acronym PERFORM.

Once the stage of development is determined, Dan told the managers, the second step would be to *determine the appropriate leadership style* needed based on the amount of directive and supportive behavior and the team's involvement in decision making. And then, finally, *specific strategies* to help the group in its development had to be determined, like clarifying roles and goals if they were unclear or teaching conflict resolution or appointing a process consultant if team members' opinions were becoming polarized.

Once specific needs have been determined Dan advised the managers to develop a specific *action plan for managing the journey* to team empowerment.

Dan created a pocket-size "Game Plan" to make it easier for the managers he taught to become effective team leaders.

TEAM DEVELOPMENT
GAME PLAN

1. Determine Purpose and Values
   Set Goals and Roles
   Build the Team Charter

Then

2. Diagnosis

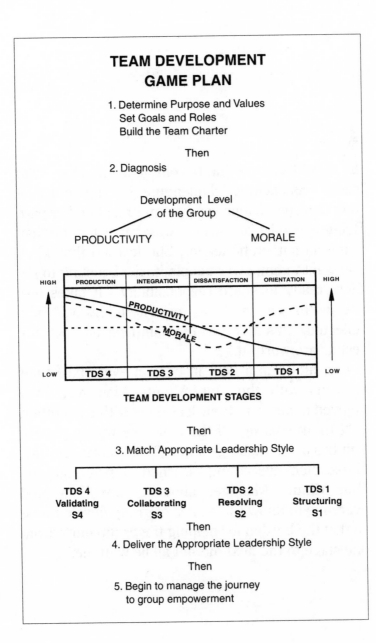

Development Level
of the Group

PRODUCTIVITY   MORALE

HIGH	PRODUCTION	INTEGRATION	DISSATISFACTION	ORIENTATION	HIGH
LOW	TDS 4	TDS 3	TDS 2	TDS 1	LOW

TEAM DEVELOPMENT STAGES

Then

3. Match Appropriate Leadership Style

TDS 4	TDS 3	TDS 2	TDS 1
Validating	Collaborating	Resolving	Structuring
S4	S3	S2	S1

Then

4. Deliver the Appropriate Leadership Style

Then

5. Begin to manage the journey
   to group empowerment

 M ARIA found that becoming an effective team leader was exciting, challenging, but not simple. It took time, persistence and commitment on her part. Being a good team leader was much harder than being an autocratic leader. She learned that when you want to empower people it is exhausting to get them ready to share responsibility. "It takes less energy to say 'my way or the highway,'" she reflected. "It's not for the fainthearted, but the results are worth it."

Dan and Maria kept in contact ever since their sessions with the One Minute Manager. They enjoyed comparing their learnings with each other.

"I think sharing all the concepts with my work unit has been the biggest help," said Maria one day. "I told them everything I learned from you and the One Minute Manager about groups. I wanted everyone to know the stages of group development so that the burden for helping the group move from one stage to the next did not all lie with me."

"Did they help with your diagnosis, too?" asked Dan.

"They sure did," answered Maria, "and it was fun too. They made comments like: 'Here we are in Stage 2!' Then once we all knew what stage the group was in, everyone helped provide the direction and support that was needed."

"I bet your folks really keep you honest, don't they?" asked Dan.

Maria smiled, "They make sure I adopt the appropriate style of leadership. But the one thing that is even more important than having my work unit involved in diagnosis and adaptability is the feeling of empowerment we all have gotten. No one is concerned if I am late or miss a meeting. They can assume leadership and I feel a new freedom and trust."

"That would really make the One Minute Manager feel happy," said Dan. "He's always told us that:

*

EMPOWERMENT

IS

ALL ABOUT

LETTING GO

SO THAT

OTHERS CAN

GET GOING

*

The End

Praisings

We would like to give credit to the following people whose conceptual contributions were invaluable to us in preparing this book.

Ken Benne and *Paul Sheats* for their pioneering work on functional roles of group members.

Paul Hersey for his creative work with Ken Blanchard in the development of Situational Leadership theory.

Irving Janis for his development and documentation of the Groupthink concept.

R. B. Lacoursiere for his thorough analysis of the life cycle of groups.

Marshall Sashkin for his courageous argument about participation as an ethical imperative.

Edgar Schein for his clear thinking about process consultation and group observation.

Jessie Stoner for her contributions to the PERFORM model.

National Training Labs Institute for its pioneering work in group dynamics and group development and for the significant impact that organization has had on all of our lives.

We are also thankful for the thoughtful reviews and critiques of:

Blanchard Consulting Partners and *University of Massachusetts* doctoral students too numerous to mention individually for their challenging and constructive feedback and suggestions.

The many participants in High Performing Team seminars and management development programs who reviewed earlier drafts of the manuscript and suggested several important changes.

About the Authors

Ken Blanchard's impact as a writer is far reaching. His bestselling book *The One Minute Manager*, coauthored with Spencer Johnson, has sold more than nine million copies worldwide and is still on bestseller lists. *The One Minute Manager* has been translated into more than twenty-five languages and is regarded as one of the most successful business books of all time. In addition, Blanchard has written several other successful books, including five more within The One Minute Manager Library. He coauthored *The Power of Ethical Management* with Dr. Norman Vincent Peale. In 1992 he released *Playing the Great Game of Golf*, followed by *Raving Fans: A Revolutionary Approach to Customer Service*, coauthored with Sheldon Bowles. In 1994 Ken released *We Are the Beloved*, a book about his spiritual journey, and in 1995 released the bestseller *Everyone's a Coach*, coauthored with Don Shula, former head coach of the Miami Dolphins. In 1996 Ken released *Empowerment Takes More Than a Minute* with Alan Randolph and John Carlos, *Managing by Values* with Michael O'Connor, and *Mission Possible: Creating a World Class Organization* with Terry Waghorn. His latest book, *Gung Ho!*, coauthored with Sheldon Bowles, is currently climbing the bestseller charts.

Ken Blanchard is chief spiritual officer of The Ken Blanchard Companies, Inc., a full-service, global management training and consulting company that he and his wife, Dr. Marjorie Blanchard, founded in 1979 in San Diego, California. He is also visiting lecturer at his alma mater, Cornell University, where he is a trustee emeritus of the Board of Trustees.

Dr. Blanchard has received several awards and honors for his contributions in the field of management, leadership, and speaking. In 1991 the National Speakers Association awarded him its highest honor, the "Council of Peers Award of Excellence." In 1992 Dr. Blanchard was inducted into the HRD Hall of Fame by *Training Magazine* and Lakewood Conferences, and he also received the 1992 Golden Gavel Award from Toastmasters International. In 1996 Ken received the Distinguished Contribution to Human Resource Development Award from the American Society of Training and Development.

Don Carew is an accomplished and respected management consultant, trainer and educator and a dynamic motivational speaker.

He has consulted with governmental, educational and business organizations throughout the United States, Mexico and Canada and specializes in the areas of leadership, team building, organization change, employee involvement and collaboration in work settings.

His addresses and seminars are presented with enthusiasm and humor and are built upon knowledge and hands-on experience. He is often regarded as genuine and caring and relates well to any audience regardless of the diversity of its members. He is a professor emeritus at the University of Massachusetts, where he directed and taught in the graduate program in organization development from 1965 to 1994.

He is a founding consulting partner with The Ken Blanchard Companies where he consults with many different organizations as well as the Blanchard Companies themselves.

He is cocreator of the High Performing Teams product line offered by The Ken Blanchard Companies and has authored a multitude of articles for professional journals. He is also an active associate of the NTL Institute.

He holds a bachelor's degree in business from Ohio University, a master's degree in human relations from Ohio University and a doctorate in counseling psychology from the University of Florida.

Eunice Parisi-Carew is an accomplished management consultant and trainer and a sought after motivational speaker.

With a broad base of experience in many facets of management and organizational development, she has designed, directed and implemented training and consulting projects for a number of top North American corporations, including Merrill Lynch, AT&T, Hyatt Hotels, Transco Energy Company and the Department of Health, Education and Welfare.

Team building, leadership, organizational change and life management are among the many topics she addresses in seminars, speeches and articles. She is also cocreator of the High Performing Teams product line offered by The Ken Blanchard Companies.

She has directed a graduate program in Group Dynamics and Leadership at the University of Hartford and was a part-time faculty member of American University. She is also a member of the Board of Directors of the NTL Institute. She has also served as vice president of Professional Services at The Ken Blanchard Companies.

She received her Ed.D. in behavioral sciences from the University of Massachusetts, and is also a licensed psychologist in the state of Massachusetts.

Currently she is a senior researcher with the Office of the Future at The Ken Blanchard Companies. Her role is to study trends that occur five to ten years out and their implications for leaders, organizations and business practices.

Services Available

The Ken Blanchard Companies comprise six business units that have been integrated into a full-service training and consulting company in the areas of team development, leadership, customer service, performance management, ethics and wellness.

Blanchard offers training services as well as a complete product line on the topic of Building High Performing Teams™ that combines the fundamentals of group dynamics with core skills of team building. This program has served as a primary benefit to organizations of every type and size in helping to increase organizational productivity through its focus upon the development of effective work teams.

Building High Performing Teams™ includes the foundation concepts of Situational Leadership® II, one of the leading management development models of our time, that will help guide your teams to maximum performance.

To find out more information about Building High Performing Teams™ or other Blanchard products, seminars or counsulting services, please call or write:

The Ken Blanchard Companies, Inc.
125 State Place, Escondido, CA 92029
(800) 728-6000 or (619) 489-5005